THE SMILING CAMEL

LORETTA ANNE ORR

Balboa Press books may be ordered through booksellers or by contacting:

Balboa Press
A Division of Hay House
1663 Liberty Drive
Bloomington, IN 47403
www.balboapress.com
1 (877) 407-4847

ISBN: 978-1-9822-2059-4 (sc)
ISBN: 978-1-9822-2058-7 (e)

Print information available on the last page.

Balboa Press rev. date: 01/24/2019

BALBOA
PRESS
A DIVISION OF HAY HOUSE

This book is dedicated to all the abused, neglected or homeless animals, and to all the fine, dedicated people who rescue, rehabilitate, house and love them.

God Bless them

I would like to thank my family and friends who supported me and helped me with this book.

Have you ever seen a camel smile? I have, but it has been awhile. The story I have to tell is true, and it happened in May at the Cincinnati Zoo.

I love animals and I am always kind, and if you are too sometimes you will find, that some of the animals will be friendly too, and respond to the things you say and do.

So, this is the story I have to tell; listen carefully and remember it well. Maybe you'll learn a thing or two about how the animals feel at the zoo.

When camels shed their winter coats, sometimes they look a fright, until their hair grows back again, and then they look all right.

When I saw the camel that day in May, she was losing her coat and kept turning away, from a family of three taking pictures of her; she didn't like it without her fur.

Animals have feelings like you and me; sad, happy, friendly or shy you see. That day the camel was feeling bad to be seen without the coat she once had. She didn't want pictures, she couldn't bear to be seen without her beautiful hair.

When the family had finished and walked away. I went up to the camel; I had to say. "I think you are beautiful, and you should not mind, being seen by others; you're a one-of-a-kind"! You should slide your leg out and lift up your head; you should stand up tall and be proud". I said.

At first the camel just turned her head and seemed not to hear what I had said.

I continued to talk so she would know how special she was, as I told her so.

I told her she had pretty eyes, and the camel came closer to my surprise. She was listening to what I had to say, and her head was no longer turned away.

The camel was near me, curious now, and I couldn't believe it or figure out how she understood what I had said; I stood in amazement shaking my head.

The camel was standing looking at me, a surprised look on her face like "this cannot be"! This lady likes me and doesn't care, if I'm shedding my coat and losing my hair.

The camel turned quickly and tossed back her head; she started to smile, and that big smile spread. Her whole face was happy as she looked at me, with her eyebrow raised; what a sight to see!

She touched my heart in such a way I will never forget my visit that day. She posed while I took a picture, and then, turned sideways and stood proudly while I took one again.

Then a moment after I was done, she turned and walked out into the sun. She did not look back, and I let her go, but the warmth in my heart continued to glow.

Be the sunlight for all the animals who need and deserve compassion and love.

All proceeds from this book will be used for the rescue, recovery, care and placement of animals in need.

Place your animal pictures here.

Printed in the United States
By Bookmasters